Singing Is a Supper, Snoopy

Selected cartoons from
THE BEAGLE HAS LANDED
Volume 3

by CHARLES M. SCHULZ

Fawcett Crest • New York

SING FOR YOUR SUPPER, SNOOPY

This book, prepared especially for Fawcett Crest Books, a unit of CBS Publications, the Consumer Publishing Division of CBS Inc., comprises a portion of THE BEAGLE HAS LANDED and is reprinted by arrangement with Holt, Rinehart and Winston, Inc.

Contents of Book: PEANUTS® comic strips by
                        Charles M. Schulz
                        Copyright © 1977, 1978 United Feature
                        Syndicate, Inc.

ISBN: 0-449-24403-2

Printed in the United States of America

First Fawcett Crest Printing: May 1981

10   9   8   7   6   5   4   3   2   1

Sing for your Supper, Snoopy

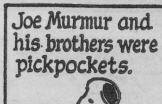

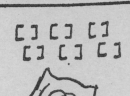

I'M PRACTICING MY BRACKETS...

DID YOU KNOW THAT BRACKETS ARE ALWAYS USED IN PAIRS?

IF YOU EVER SEE A BRACKET BY ITSELF, YOU CAN BE SURE IT'S UP TO NO GOOD!

OKAY, NOW HERE'S WHAT YOU DID WRONG...

I KNOW WHAT I DID WRONG! I NEVER SHOULD HAVE SPOKEN TO YOU YEARS AGO! I NEVER SHOULD HAVE LET YOU INTO MY LIFE! I SHOULD HAVE WALKED AWAY! I SHOULD HAVE TOLD YOU TO GET LOST! THAT'S WHAT I DID WRONG, YOU BLOCKHEAD!!

YOU ALSO PROBABLY SHOULD HOLD YOUR HANDS A LITTLE CLOSER TOGETHER...

YOU KNOW WHAT?

I THINK I'VE LEARNED THE SECRET OF LIFE...

I WENT TO THE DOCTOR YESTERDAY BECAUSE I HAD A SORE THROAT...THE NURSE PUT ME IN A SMALL ROOM..

➤

IF YOU WERE A REAL OWL, YOU KNOW WHAT YOU'D DO?

YOU'D SWOOP OUT OF YOUR TREE, AND CATCH A MOUSE

THAT'S WHAT YOU'D DO IF YOU WERE A REAL OWL

THAT'S WHAT I'D DO IF I WERE OUT OF MY MIND!

HERE WE ARE...

NOW, THIS WILL BE SORT OF A REHEARSAL FOR TOMORROW NIGHT, SNOOPY...

TOMORROW IS HALLOWEEN, AND ON HALLOWEEN NIGHT THE GREAT PUMPKIN RISES OUT OF THE PUMPKIN PATCH, AND BRINGS TOYS TO ALL THE CHILDREN IN THE WORLD...

YOUR JOB IS TO BE KIND OF A PAUL REVERE...WHEN THE GREAT PUMPKIN COMES, YOU'LL GET ON YOUR HORSE, AND RIDE THROUGH THE COUNTRYSIDE SPREADING THE NEWS!

OKAY, LET'S REHEARSE IT..

HE'S COMING! HE'S COMING! THE GREAT PUMPKIN IS COMING!

RIDE, SNOOPY, RIDE! SPREAD THE NEWS!

I FEEL LIKE SUCH A FOOL!

TONIGHT IS HALLOWEEN, ISN'T IT, LINUS?

I'VE DECIDED I NEED SOMETHING TO BELIEVE IN SO I'M GOING TO SIT HERE WITH YOU, AND WAIT!

I WANT TO SEE THE "GREAT GRAPE" WHEN HE ARRIVES...

"PUMPKIN"! SORRY

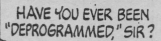
HAVE YOU EVER BEEN "DEPROGRAMMED," SIR?

IT'S TERRIBLE! MY FAMILY HAS BEEN YELLING AT ME ALL NIGHT...

APPARENTLY IT'S ALL RIGHT TO BELIEVE IN SANTA CLAUS, BUT IT'S WRONG TO BELIEVE IN THE "GREAT GRAPE"

I THINK THAT'S "PUMPKIN," MARCIE...

I'M STILL FEELING A LITTLE DIZZY...

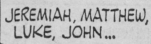

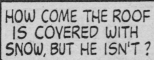
I DON'T UNDERSTAND..

HOW COME THE ROOF IS COVERED WITH SNOW, BUT HE ISN'T?

SNOW DOES NOT STICK TO A WARM, CUDDLY BODY!

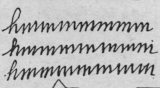

I'VE NEVER GOTTEN A GOLD STAR FOR ANYTHING, MARCIE

THE TEACHER GIVES GOLD STARS FOR SPELLING, FOR ATTENDANCE, FOR DRINKING MILK AND FOR EVERYTHING, BUT I NEVER GET A GOLD STAR!

HAVE YOU EVER GOTTEN A GOLD STAR, MARCIE?

I GOT ONE FOR SPELLING, ONE FOR ATTENDANCE, ONE FOR DRINKING MILK, ONE FOR..

FORGET IT, MARCIE!

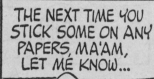

YOU LOOK SMALLER TODAY, SIR, AND YOU SEEM QUIETER....

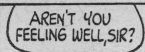

AREN'T YOU FEELING WELL, SIR?

WHAT KIND OF ILLNESS MAKES YOUR BODY SHRINK BUT YOUR NOSE GET BIGGER?

LOOK WHAT I FOUND IN YOUR WASTEBASKET, MISS TENURE... YOUR BOX OF GOLD STARS!

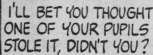

I'LL BET YOU THOUGHT ONE OF YOUR PUPILS STOLE IT, DIDN'T YOU?

THEY WOULDN'T DO ANYTHING LIKE THAT... ESPECIALLY THAT CUTE ONE WITH THE BEAUTIFUL HAIR AND THE FRECKLES..

YOU KNOW WHAT YOU SHOULD DO ON BEETHOVEN'S BIRTHDAY?

YOU SHOULD TAKE ME OUT TO DINNER...

I WOULDN'T TAKE YOU TO A BUBBLE-GUM CHEW!

YOU WOULDN'T?

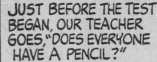

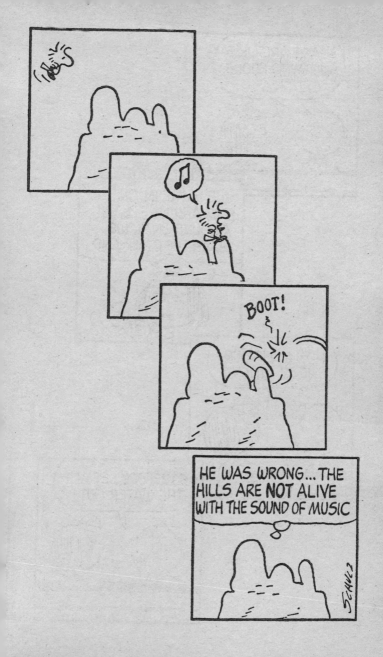

OKAY, BEAUTIFUL, GET OFF THE ICE!! WE'RE GONNA PLAY HOCKEY!

HOCKEY?! GET LOST, NECKHEAD! I WAS HERE FIRST!!

YOU WOULDN'T LIKE TO GET HIT WITH A HOCKEY STICK WOULD YOU, BEAUTIFUL?

HOW WOULD YOU LIKE TO BE FORCE-FED A PAIR OF GOALIE PADS?!

LISTEN, BEAUTIFUL, GET YOUR STUPID FIGURE SKATES OFF THE ICE! WE WANNA PLAY HOCKEY, SEE?

WE HAVE TEN HOCKEY STICKS HERE TELLING YOU TO "GET OFF THE ICE!"

OH, YEAH? COME ON AND TRY SOMETHING! ME AND MY COACH'LL TAKE YOU ALL ON!!

I THINK I'LL GO HOME.. I HAVE SOME CHAIN LETTERS TO WRITE...

GUESS WHAT, SIR..WHEN I GOT HOME AND TOLD MY MOTHER ABOUT FALLING ON THE ICE SHE CALLED THE DOCTOR...

HE TOLD YOU TO TAKE IT EASY HUH? WELL, THAT MAKES SENSE..CAN I GET YOU ANYTHING?

NO, THANK YOU, SIR... I'M JUST GOING TO LIE HERE, AND TRY TO READ "PILGRIM'S PROGRESS"

IF THE FALL ON THE ICE DIDN'T GIVE YOU A CONCUSSION, MARCIE, THAT WILL!

I'M AFRAID I'M GOING TO BE A DISAPPOINTMENT TO YOU, MARCIE...

I WENT OVER TO THE RINK TODAY TO GET REVENGE ON THOSE HOCKEY PLAYERS

DID YOU PUNCH THEIR LIGHTS OUT, SIR?

I WAS GOING TO, MARCIE...

BUT THEN THEY ASKED ME TO PLAY CENTER ON THEIR TEAM!

SCHULZ

OOPS! SORRY, MA'AM!
I GUESS I DOZED
OFF FOR A SECOND

I DREAMED I HAD
JUST BEEN GIVEN A
SCHOLARSHIP TO VASSAR

WELL, BACK
TO REALITY!

NOW IF SOME KID COMES UP, AND STARTS ASKING ABOUT A RULER, YOU HOLD HIM OFF...

HOLD HIM OFF?

YES, YOU HOLD HIM OFF WHILE I RUN FOR IT!

WHAT IF HE TRIES TO HIT ME?

REASON WITH HIM

TELL HIM HIS STUPID RULER WOULDN'T HAVE BEEN ANY GOOD AFTER WE SWITCHED TO METRICS, ANYWAY!

AND JUST AS I WAS MEASURING THE WIDTH OF THE STREET IN FRONT OF OUR SCHOOL, A TRUCK RAN OVER THE RULER...

SO MUCH FOR MY REPORT ON IMPROVED TRAFFIC CONTROL

WHAT ABOUT MY RULER?

IGNORE HIM, MA'AM.. HE HAS A ONE-TRACK MIND!

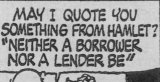

MAY I QUOTE YOU SOMETHING FROM HAMLET? "NEITHER A BORROWER NOR A LENDER BE"

WHAT'S THAT SUPPOSED TO MEAN?

IT MEANS YOU SHOULDN'T HAVE BORROWED THAT KID'S RULER IN THE FIRST PLACE! MAKES YOU THINK, DOESN'T IT?

YOU HATE ME, DON'T YOU?

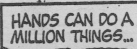

MORE PEANUTS®

☐ SNOOPY, TOP DOG
   (selected cartoons from
   The Beagle Has Landed, Vol. 2)   24373 $1.75

☐ JOGGING IS IN, SNOOPY
   (selected cartoons from
   The Beagle Has Landed, Vol. 1)   24344 $1.50

☐ STAY WITH IT, SNOOPY!
   (selected cartoons from
   Summers Walk, Winters Fly, Vol. 3)   24310 $1.50

☐ YOU'RE A PAL, SNOOPY!
   (selected cartoons from
   You Need Help, Charlie Brown, Vol. 2)   23775 $1.25

☐ PLAY BALL, SNOOPY
   (selected cartoons from
   Win a Few, Lose a Few, Charlie Brown, Vol. 1) 23222 $1.50

☐ HERE'S TO YOU, CHARLIE BROWN
   (selected cartoons from
   You Can't Win, Charlie Brown, Vol. 2)   23708 $1.50

Buy them at your local bookstore or use this handy coupon for ordering.

COLUMBIA BOOK SERVICE (a CBS Publications Co.)
32275 Mally Road, P.O. Box FB, Madison Heights, MI 48071
Please send me the books I have checked above. Orders for less than 5 books must include 75¢ for the first book and 25¢ for each additional book to cover postage and handling. Orders for 5 books or more postage is FREE. Send check or money order only.

Cost $_____	Name_____
Sales tax*_____	Address_____
Postage_____	City_____
Total $_____	State_____ Zip_____

*The government requires us to collect sales tax in all states except AK, DE, MT, NH and OR.

This offer expires 1 January 82   8170